NOT MORE!

TO SHOUT C

by Ernest Henry

To Sylvia; to Kleshna

First published in Great Britain in 1997
Bloomsbury Publishing Plc, 38 Soho Square, London W1V 5DF

A CIP catalogue record of this book is available from the British Library

ISBN 0 7475 3433 0

Printed in Great Britain by
Clays Ltd., St. Ives plc

10 9 8 7 6 5 4 3 2

NOT MORE!?! *POEMS TO SHOUT OUT LOUD*

by Ernest Henry

BLOOMSBURY

CONTENTS

Not More!?! Poems to Shout out Loud

SECTION ONE

Poems to . . .

Poems to . . .

Poems to . .

I'M JUST A LITTLE KID, WAITING TO GET OUT!

(Boom, Boom, Boom, Boom!)

I'd like to thump around and make a smashing noise.
I'd like to dash about and play with metal toys.
But I'm stuck in my pen gurgling all about:
I'm just a little kid waiting to get out!

I'd like to climb the stairs and reach the very top.
I wanna ride the dog and never, never stop.
I'd like to split the pen, and shake it all about:
I'm just a little kid waiting to get out!

I'm sick of cuddly toys and tinny music boxes;
I'm tired of teddy bears and dolls like Goldilockses;
I want those toys with a sharp pointed corner –
I don't want no nursery rhymes about Little Jack Horner.

I'm sick of videos 'bout Toy Town and the rest.
Want a movie with Bruce Willis in his vest.
I want some music where the singers scream and shout:
I'm just a little kid waiting to get out!

I'm tired of baby clothes and jamas fulls of bears.
I wanna wear my studs and get into some flares.
I'd like to split this pen, and shake it all about:
I'm just a little kid waiting to get out!

I need to eat a meal that's rich and very yummy,
That's sweet and full of goo and fills my little tummy.
I'd like some steak and chips but I can't chew: I'm gummy.
I want Pamela Anderson for my mummy!!

Why can't the grown ups talk properly to me?
What is wrong with all their vo-ca-bu-la-ry?
I'm with the Spider – I'm going up the spout!
I'm just a little kid waiting to get out!

I Don't Know Why . . .

I don't know why –
My Mum goes popping wozzy in the morning when I'm all geared up getting ready for another wonderful day at school – Not!!

I don't know why –
My Mum stromps into my bedroom at five to eight in the morning while I'm happily snoozling cosy warm inside upside-down duvet and pillows completely out of it all.

I don't know why –
My Mum yells "What-are-you-still-doing-in-bed – it's FIVE-TO-EIGHT-and you're not up" when it's obvious I'm not up . . . yet, but I'm preparing mentally for the difficult tasks of the day ahead . . .

. . . Like washing my teeth –
. . . And brushing my hair.

I don't know why –
My Mum strimms like a top, steam fuming out of her ears as she cooks the brekky full of saussi, eggie-bakie, toast 'n marm and hot chocolate while rushing around the place thundering –

"Wash hands face and teeth.
Put your shoes on.
Where's your school bag?
Where's your homework?
Why can't you find your pen?
Brush your hair – it's a mess.
Have you washed? HAVE you washed?
    No you haven't – go and wash.
Where's your music?
What do you mean you've only one shoe?
Have you practiced behind your ears?
Comb your teeth,
Tie your hair,
Finish your eggs,
Put on your sausage and
    GO TO SCHOOL!!"

I don't know why.

I mean – I was going to
    do that anyway.

Right?

Whadyathinkathat?

I've got a bike
With great treads,
Forty two gears,
Two sirens,
Twin headlights at the front
AND sequential lights at the back.
Whadyathinkathat, John?

I've got a pair of blades
With two hydraulic brake
systems,
Power steering,
Built in radar,
Indicators
And thermonuclear tootsie
warmers.
Whadyathinkathat, Jack?

I've got a skate-board
With cruise control,
Auto slip-stream guidance
integration,
Auto weave adjusters,
Auto dbs brake system,
Auto auto
Whadyathinkathat, Jane?

Yeah? Well –
I've got a human assimilation unit
With stereophonic sound receivers,
Instant audio playback,
Adjustable digitalisation,
Quadro-hydraulic
manipulation,
Thirty nine external
facia modes,
Accesorisation for
twenty separate
integrated
modular systems,
Personal terrestrial transporter unit
AND it can cry and wee at the same time!
Whadyathinkathat?

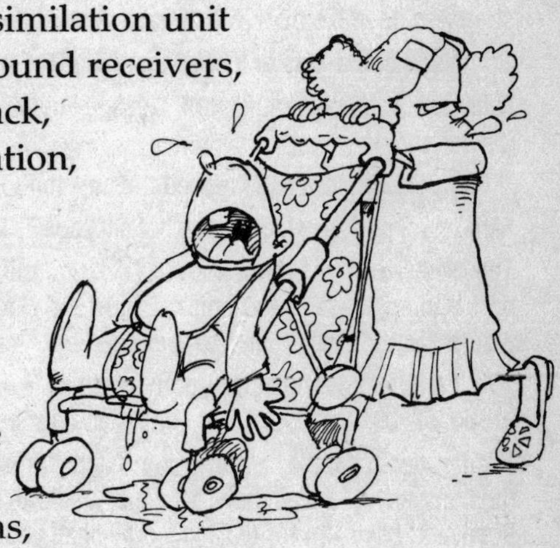

The Sausage

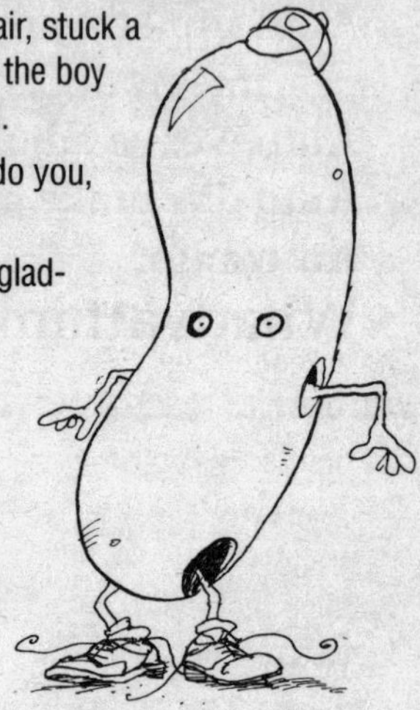

The Old Schoolmaster swung back on his swivel chair, stuck a digit up his left nostril and glared across his desk at the boy nervously picking the cuticles around his thumb nail.

"So you think you're good enough to be a sausage do you, laddie," ventured the Wrinkled One.

"Oh yes – I do," said the boy earnestly wisting with glad-happy eyes.

"You don't see yourself as an egg, perchance, or even a baked bean," inquired the Teacher.

"No, no. I don't." The boy was emphatic. "I'm definitely a sausage."

"Right!" declared the Teach after a moment's pause in the proceedings.

"One sausage equals Biggs." And he wrote the strange note in his book with great solemnity.

On finishing, the Master looked up and gazed intently at the boy once again.

"May one enquire what kind of sausage you'd consider yourself?" asked the Master.

"I beg your pardon, sir?" replied the boy, innocent eyes open wide.

"Are you a pork sausage, or a beef sausage?" The boy was unable to answer.

The Master continued impatiently. "Are you mixed herbs and spices, peppered, pork and apple, sage and onion, Laurel and Hardy, Marks and Spencer – what type are you?" The Master banged the desk.

"Oh, I suppose I'd be a plain pork sausage, like the sort you have for your breakfast, sir," the boy at last understanding the question.

"Impertinent chappie," intoned the Teach, "presupposing that I"d be seen dead in the company of a plain pork sausage, let alone eat one in the morning for my breakfast. I like 'em for tea. How pray shall you be cooked?"

"Oh, fried," replied the boy, considering the answer carefully. 'Yes, definitely fried."

"I see," remarked the Teach. "Fried – in butter – slowly so as to be cooked through to the middle. A deep glaze on your skin. With a tomato or two?" asked the Teacher.

The boy nodded.

"And when you're cooked, and ready, how would you like to be served?" asked the Master, relishing the thought his mind was conjuring up.

"On a plate," replied the boy.

"Alone?" inquired the Master, "Or would you consider having a friendly egg or two, baked bean and of course tomato along for company?"

"Oh, not alone," replied the boy. "Everything on the plate at the same."

"Everything on the plate at the same time. Messy Mutant!" The Master scrunched up his face and noted the modus servus in his mysterious book.

The Teach set down his pen, leant back in his chair, his fingers pressed together, and asked the boy, "Now as to eating. Would you like to be sliced long-wise with one bold stoke of the knife splitting you, as it were, from north to south."

The boy rustled uncomfortably in his seat.

"Or would you prefer to be diced up in lots of neat little round bite-sized segments – chop, chop, chop?" Teach's eyes bulged eagerly as he made little chopping movements with his right hand. The boy could swear he could see the Master's mouth salivating.

"Well – er – I think, either way, sir." replied the boy unsure now as exactly what to say anymore, his vivid imagination running away with him, the Master turning into some ghastly ghoul at every moment, his fate that of every horror movie victim.

"*Sliced either way*" wrote down the Master in his book, glancing up at the boy a couple of times as he did so, after which he leant back in his chair again.

"Right, Biggs," said the Master after another thoughtful pause, long enough to cause the boy more discomfort and a short sharp shock at the breaking silence.

"You Are Now A Sausage. So you better tell your Mum – I presume you have one of those, laddie? – to make you a Sausage Costume so that you can appear in the School Play next month."

"Oh righto, sir," replied the boy, relieved he wasn't in some horror pic after all – just in the room of the Old Schoolmaster. A funny bloke, to be sure. But simply Old Teach, nonetheless. He got up from his chair, went to the door, opened it and left the room.

As he closed the door, he could hear the Old Schoolmaster cackling – "Sausage? Sausage? Chop-Chop-Chop. Chop-Chop-Chop! Yum-Yum-Yum!" Then peels of maniacal laughter . . .

CURFEW THE KIDS

The Minister said "Raise income!
And let's not be weak-willed or lax:
When a child reaches ten
That should be when
The child should start paying us tax!"

"Never!" replied the back benchers,
"Are you mad – you'll just sink the boat.
Let's find a way
To make the kids pay
Er – without losing every vote!"

And that's how the idea was vested
To curfew our kids at age ten.
You'll inquire, of course, who
Could possibly do
This Job For Stout-Hearted Men?

'Traffic Wardens' has been suggested.
They'd surely be up to the mark.
Imagine the scene
When our early teen
Is caught in the street after dark.

Rows of kids are stranded on pavements,
Each clamped in iron hoof –
With fines stuck on their foreheads
And signs on their chests – Don't Remove!

And people would pass them with pity,
Helpless. Now here's the rub:
'Cause there they must stay until someone
Arrives from the Kid Clamping Club.

Let us dwell on the drama
As the Kid Clamping Unit Swoops,
And Mum rushes out in pyjama
With excuses and turning of hoops:

"Don't clamp him," she pleads, "he's a baby!"
But the Unit man's deaf – like his ilk.
"I only sent him to the corner shop
To bring back a bottle of milk!"

What if the fines are unpaid?
Is there wailing from near and far?
Are kid's permanently grounded,
Locked and impounded
Together with Clamped Up Car?

. . . I somehow don't think it's a winner
And suggest Government put it to bed.
Perhaps they should target the aged,
And clamp every zimmer instead.

I Only Asked!!

It was a lovely sunny morning. Saturday. There was no school so I got up!

I looked out of the window at the day and saw our car.

"I know," I thought. "I'll clean Dad's car!"

"Can I, Dad, can I?"

"What?" Huh! Eh! Grunt!!" Dad babbled on.

"Can I clean the car?"

"Do-you-know what-time-it-is? he replied from somewhere underneath piles of pillows.

"No," I said.

"It's FIVE THIRTY IN THE MORNING. Go – go – do whatever you want – just let me sleep!"

"I only asked," I said, but I was out of the house in a flash, hose on, rubber gloves, gallons of soapy stuff and two huge sponges.

WHHOOOSH!! went the water out of the hose and I squirted washing liquid all over the car. You need to use a lot to clean such a big thing.

The sponges foamed up and soon there were huge mountains of bubbles all over the place.

It was great.

"WHAT ARE YOU DOING," Dad's voice boomed from his upstairs window.

"Hallo," I said looking up, waving, hose in hand. Unfortunately, water whoosshed straight up knocking Dad over with the force.

Mum appeared at the door and I swung around to see what she wanted.

It wasn't my fault water whoosshed past her too, straight into the hall, soaking the cat.

And was it my fault the milkman slipped on the soapy sludge in the driveway, breaking all his bottles and getting soaked?

And it's not my fault Dad didn't close the windows of the car last night and the inside was full of water, like a bath.

And it's c-e-r-t-a-i-n-l-y not my fault Dad got soaked (again – he-he!) as he opened the car door to get in.

After all . . .

I only asked!

SECTION TWO

RO - LY POE - LI'S

ARE WE NEARLY THERE YET?

Are we nearly there yet?
Are we nearly there yet?
Are we nearly there yet?
Are we nearly there yet?

Travelling in the car
Can be awfully boring
Dad is busy driving
Wish that Mum was snoring.
The Baby's being sick
My little brother's being naughty
He oughtn't to be, ought he?
Are we nearly there?

Here's another town
Full of busy high streets
Dad is grumbling why streets
Have to be so jammed.
Mum puts on a grunge
And shakes her head again. "We
Should have gone by train!"
Are we nearly there?

At last we're in the country
The road is whizzing past now
Dad is driving fast now
Mum squirms in her seat:
"You're going over fifty.
You should be doing forty!"
Dad says something naughty.
Are we nearly there?

The petrol's getting low:
Mum starts a massive wozzee
Screams at Dad because 'e
Should have filled the car.
My brother drops his sarney.
Mum does really barmey,
Dad wished he'd joined the army!
Are we nearly there?

Soon we're on the motorway
Eating up the miles
Everybody smiles.
Not too far to go –
When my little brother says he
Needs to do a wee-wee
Dad says something naughty and ". . . can't he
Wait – *we're nearly there!"*

He can't – it's a disaster:
The back seat's wet and soggy,
Smells like ancient doggy,
Dad says he just can't stop!
We open all the windows
And everywhere the wind blows
Bits of maps and tisshose
Are we nearly there?

At last we reach the hotel
And tumble from the car
Dad rushes for the bar
Mum goes to check us in.
But the man says we're too early
We were expected Monday
Today is only Sunday.
Mum says "But that's just ONE day!"
The man replies that Monday
Is Monday, not Sunday.
So come back on Monday
And our rooms will be there!

Back in the car
The atmosphere is fizzing
Mum is purple, quizzing
Dad – who'd got it wrong.
We're ALL feeling sick now
What a horrid outing
Can no-one hear me shouting
Are we nearly there?

On My Dad's Shoulder

I've travelled the world on my Dad's shoulder,
And the only problem with getting older
Is when I'm too big to straddle his head
I'll have to walk,
Myself,
Instead.

TO BE (OR NOT TO BE)

2B or not 2B:
That is the question.

'Cause if it were 2C
The car in Figure three
Couldn't reach the tree
Because of the congestion.

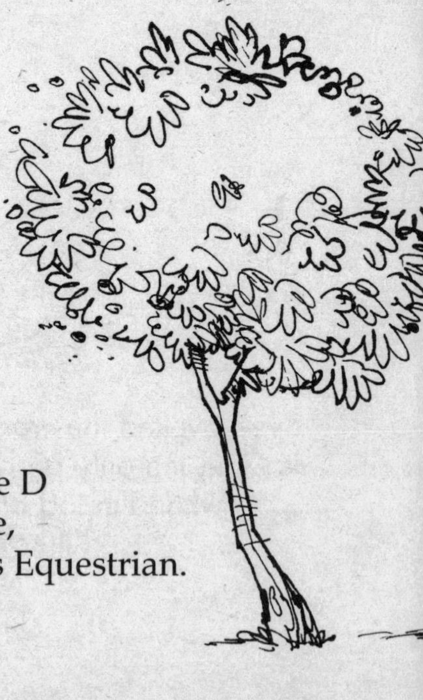

But if it were 2B
The girl in Picture D
Riding on her gee,
Could, as she was Equestrian.

Figure 3

Picture D

Postcard From Malibu

Oh what a fuss
What a to-do:
We're visiting cousins
In Malibu.

All sorts of stars
Of film and TV
Lie on the beach
Or swim in the sea,

Run to the shops,
Sit in cafes,
Eager as ants
To soak up the rays

So they'll bronze
And be glam as can be,
And picked to appear
On national TV.

Our cousin Bertie's
Been on the box
Wearing his bowler
And bright yellow socks.

In fact he's seen
Five times a week
On his own show
"Gerbils Must Squeak!!"

Malibu's fun
Though it does slip and slide
And houses are often
Washed away with the tide!

But it's busy and bustling
And quite a delight,
Except for the cars
That drive on the right:

Very confusing
When crossing the road.
Why, I had to get help
From a passing toad!

Well, that's all from us,
We have to go.
We're being called now
To appear on a show!

There we were,
Minding our P's,
Sunning our tails,
When, if you please

This chap from the tele
Said we'd caught his eye
And would we be filmed,
Nera and I!!

Well, you can imagine
We couldn't agree –
Until, that is,
He mentioned the fee!

So watch your TV's
No, it's not Morse:
We've joined the Babes
In Baywatch, of course!

THE PEN!

The Pen lay between index and thumb
Waiting for something worth writing to come.
Ink poised to drain away,
Nib glinting gold in the cold light of day . . .

Thick and black it shone in the night
While the Hand that held it attempted to write . . .
Morning arrived, and still not a line
Had been scribbled by Pen. Was it a sign?

With impatient disgust Pen gazed up
at the writer
Who, he considered, <u>had</u> looked much
brighter:
Eyes weary red and drooping of lid,
Stubble and grey, shirt collar undid;
Slime sweaty fingers and clammy palm,
Limp of head, of body and arm.

"Right!" Said Pen, the diagnosis done
"He's got The Block – better give him
one."
Major shock, that is: that's what
pen's do
When writers who use them
haven't a clue.

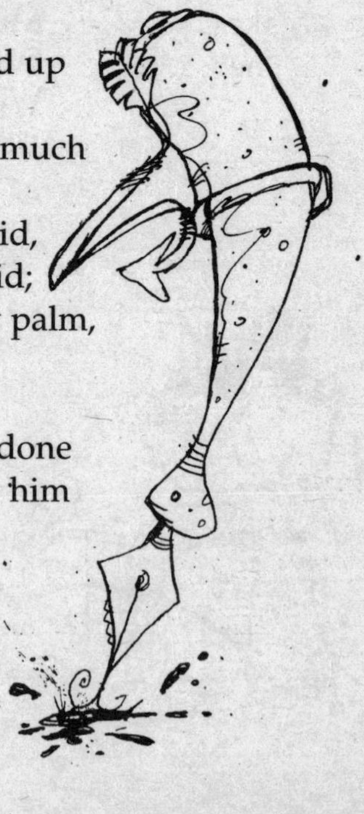

"Heeeeaaave!!" Went Pen, with enormous strain
Producing a BLOB!, an indelible stain.
"That should do it!" And indeed it did:
Jumping five feet, knocking over his chair
Which landed on Dog who'd been snoozling there,
The writer's foot buckled as he hit the ground
And snapped at the joint with a hollow sound,
And he fell on his table knocking all to the floor,
Squashed the Cat and slid through the door
Where he bashed his head on the handle of brass
Which knocked him out cold.

And it came to pass
That while he was out – out like a light,
He had a dream which he thought just might
Make a good story to earn him a crumb
So he wrote:

'The Pen lay between index and thumb . . .'

COLONEL GUM

His name is Colonel Gum
Moustache and rounded tum
He'd keep his teeth together
Whatever was to come.

The Molar trek was rough
Toothpicks weren't enough
Because of the awful weather
The going would be tough.

They trudged around the gums,
The Colonel and his chums
To rid themselves of Sugar
And other Foreign Crumbs.

"We could've used the tube,"
The Wisdom Tooth ensued.
But the Colonel shouted *"Never!!!*
And don't be bloody rude!"

"We need you sparkling white."
The Colonel screamed all night.
"We're marching on for ever!"
His plaque was worse than his bite.

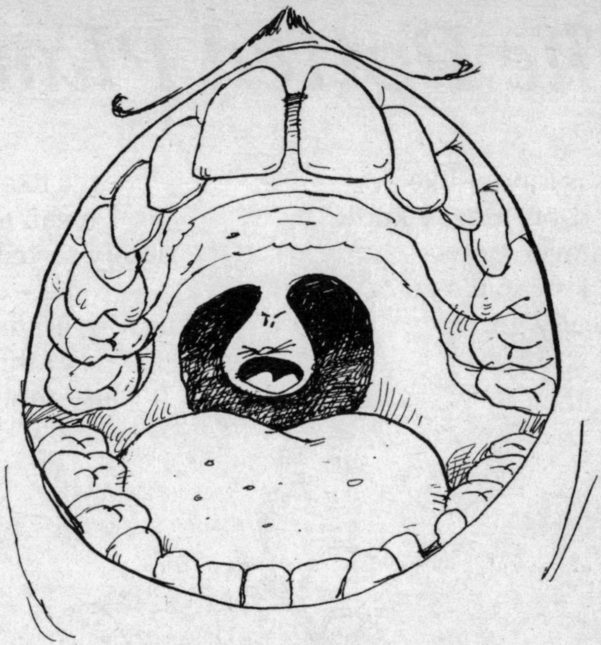

"Why not floss instead
Of marching 'till we're dead,"
The back teeth moaned together
"Life's hanging by a thread!"

"Piffle juice and tar."
The Colonel yelled afar,
"Better this than fillings!
Keep together nar!!"

His name was Colonel Gum
Moustache and rounded tum
He'd keep his teeth together
Whatever was to come.

The Potted Plant

This is kind-a-like
A sort-of-thing, y'know.
Whatever, um –
    I mean it's gotta
Basically grow –

It's like well
I mean to say
Mainly sorted and
it's – er . . .
Anyway, at the end
of the day
It's just another –
y'know.

One morning Sarah went out
Wondering what all the fuss was about
She breathed in a sigh
And stared at the sky
When she saw Morag fly by

by Geri Jones age 10

SECTION THREE

Rrrrrrrrrrrrrrrrrrrrrrriggelivvordssssssssssssssssss

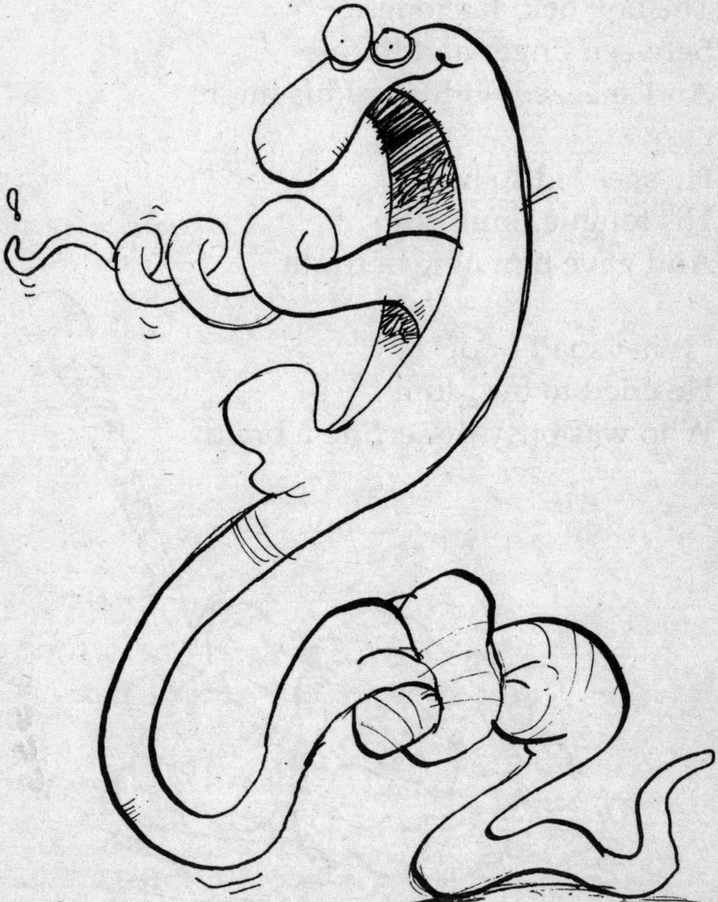

THE TONGUE

(To be spoken . . . out loud . . . while holding your tongue between thumb and finger!)

The boy held his tongue
Between finger and thumb
And sneezed with all of his might.

He sneezed so hard
His tongue came out
And gave him quite a fright.

"What shall I do?"
He cried to his Mum
Who was busy dissecting a brain:

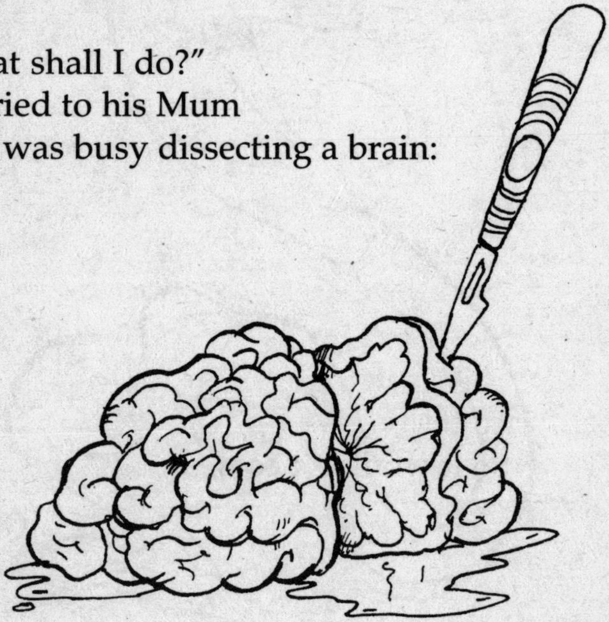

She sewed it back on
To his bottom lip,
So it wouldn't come out again!

THE FELLA FROM READING

There was this young fella from Reading
Who got lost in a mountain of bedding.
They found his pyjamas
In the Bahamas
Being worn by a bride at her wedding!

THE FRENCH TEACHER

Throaty rrrr's and "ons" and "eins",
Elastic lips and floaty hands,
Strangulating words with sighs,
Heaving shoulders, popping eyes . . .

The teachers who will wring and wrench
Their bodies just to teach us French
Are altogether quite unique –
Especially when they start to speak . . .

They talk of Jean and Jeanne-Marie,
Of coffee breaks instead of tea,
And times of trains from Nice to Nantes,
The cost of cakes, and Anna's Aunt . . .

Shopping lists and when it rains,
Traffic jams and clogged up drains,
Visits here and travels there,
Where to go and what to wear . . .

Immersed they are in verbs and tense,
The dog who jumps the garden fence.
They weigh tomatoes one by one
And never seem to have much fun!

When at last the lesson's done
We pack our French books, one by one.
Leave the class and Teacher too
Still mouthing "ee and o and ou!

Oh la la and allez-op!"
They wheel and whirr just like a top
Shrugging "ouff" and "allez-y"
While we pretend we cannot see
The smoking shoes, the fizzing hair,
The gnarling teeth, the distant stare,
Steam erupting from the ears
As Teacher violently disappears
Waving now in Gallic mime
Back in the French Book until next time.

THE FELLA FROM EALING

There was an old fella from Ealing
Who saw an elephant dance on the ceiling!
He wondered why
It wasn't a fly
And why the ceiling was peeling!

THE DENTIST FROM GLOUCESTER

The Dentist from Gloucester was glum
Because of the boil on his bum.
He wanted to lance it,
But just wouldn't chance it
Because of the sore on his thumb.

THE AUL BLOKE

"Comme jhere", sayded the Aul Bloke Perjionman to the Littelchappeliething who toddled over and ogelled up at the whiskery whispy visog with startlingly large nosey holes full of hairy bits.

"Whatja wanting mee for," sayded the Littelchappeliething.

"I's cantey movee me leggy bits at a cause of the Black Crow, cursed be his venticlaus. 'E picked and pecked at me knee joints whilst I's took me snooziness at the lasted Darkitude, and now I's have holy knee caps what take in the waters from the grey whispies in the sky."

"That be shockin terrible," avered the Littelchappeliething, moving up closer to the Aul Bloke Perjionman perched on his rock overlooking the valley below.

"Yesti, yesti," sighded the Aul Bloke.

"Can I's ogle the knee bits what the Black Crow, cursed be his venticlaus, left you," enquired the Littelchappeliething, full of curiositude.

"Do you's really wanting to," asked the Aul Bloke, nosey holes twitching and glistening.

"Oh yesti, yesti," replied the Littelchappeliething, eagering with every time bit that passed.

"Very well," sayded the Aul Bloke rolling down his leggy pipings showing his knee.

"Look closest now," he proposed, and the Littelchappeliething moved closest as can be.

But the Littelchappeliething sawed nothing, cos the Aul Bloke bent down his whiskery whispy visog and cheweded oft the Littelchappeliething's head in one go.

"Um," contemplated the Aul Bloke, then sighded with the jolly-of-it-all. "No matter what I's does to heducate the folksies, them Littelchappeliethings are still allowed to wandering all over the place."

And the Aul Bloke Perjionman burped a sad burp and waited for the next vic-pupil to come along.

SECTION FOUR

DARKSTY MOODIES

SUCCESS?

Darksty moodies,
Grim forebodings,
Angst and gut-crunching, brow-knitted traum.

Laughing lightly,
Brightly – frightly,
Hiding the storm brooding since he was born.

Wary weary.
Stealing glances.
Oniony fear through his nostrils flared.

Watchful waiting.
Stealing chances
No others took – but only he dared.

I'M SICK!!

I'm sick in bed – I've got the flu.
And guess what: it's the weekend too.
I've gargled and sprayed the back of me throat,
I'm sniffing and wheezing. I cough like a goat,
And phlegm's flying all over the place
When I roar out a sneeze which explodes from me face.
And I ache –
              and I pain –
                            – and me head feels rotten.
And I'm sure me friends have all forgotten
Me lying here . . .
              Dying . . .
                     Alone . . .

Mum!!

I'VE BEEN TO THE EDGE OF THE WORLD AND BACK

I'vd been to the Edge Of The World and back,
I've seen right over the side,
Where the lines are long
With a shuffling throng
And there's nowhere you can hide.

Where life is a number, a ticket a code,
Eyes are hollowed and backs are bowed
And for many a soul it's a one-way road.
I've been to the Edge Of The World.

I've been to the Edge Of The World and back,
I've seen right over the side,
Where the smell of the air
Is thick with despair
And it's hard to show courage and pride.

Where the past is grim and the future looks bleak;
You try to be strong, but your voice is weak
And your throat is so dry your tongue clings to your cheek.
I've been to the Edge Of The World.

I've been to the Edge Of The World and back,
I've seen right over the side.
And despite the cold night
A glimmering light
Shone dimly as if to chide:

"Down through the ages, Man's fallen to rise:
His life lived in trying, not tearful goodbyes!"
So I'll pull up me socks, and do up me flies –
I'm back from the Edge Of
The World.

THE ROOM WE WERE IN
(Kept On Groaning Away . . .)

Sad, mad Mary, Sally and me
Sat in a corner sipping some tea.
I understood not a word they would say
As the room we were in kept on groaning
 away . . .

Sighs from eyes interred in stone;
And moans of monosyllabic tone
Came from Old Pieces with nothing
 to say
As the room we were in kept on
 groaning away . . .

Tea cups rattled attempting to
 play
With saucers awash in the
 milky grey;
But the Pieces continued to
 sit and to stay
As the room we were in
 kept on groaning away . . .

Sad, mad Mary, Sally and me
Sat in a corner sipping some tea.
I've left them both now, but remember the day
The room we were in kept on groaning away . . .

THE LIE

There was once this Lie. It was a very little, sweet, blonde Lie. An ever-so-cosy-rosy-round-the-door sort of Lie. And the Lie didn't do any harm to anybody. In fact, quite the opposite. People used to ooh and aah at the things the Lie would come out with.

"What a joker," they'd say. "What imagination! Whatever will it think of next," they'd beam in admiration, almost.

And the Lie would smile sweetly, proud and happy.

As the Lie grew, it came to believe some of the stories it told and that no matter what was actually said, the people would believe them too – well almost. So the Lie became more creative, not really by choice, but now, by necessity. Because the Lie came to realise that it liked being liked and could get what it wanted just by lying. It couldn't stand the thought of being discovered and caught out by all its admiring fans for what it truly was – just a lie.

So the Lie had to become more inventive, and as time passed, more inventive still.

It grew and grew and the stories became more

involved, one having to match another, one set of circumstances having to fit snugly into what had been said before.

And it became complicated. It also started to become harder. Because as the Lie grew, the people who had once admired and applauded, became suspicious, questioning all that had been told to them before.

So the Lie had to keep growing. never stopping, always expanding upon the stories . . . and to more and more people, too.

Soon, very soon, some of the people began talking together and discussing the Lie and all that it'd been saying. And the Lie had to start twisting and turning, shifting and squirming in order just to keep going.

At night, the Lie couldn't sleep, lying awake trying to remember, trying to remember what 'ad been said to whom and when and why! Would it never end? No! Not until the Lie was dead, would it ever end.

And soon the Lie became uglier, because that's how it is with Lies. And the stories came thick and fast and started to hurt people. Instead of being amused and beaming, the people started baying and snarling, threatening and screaming: banging-on-his-door-in-the-middle-of-the-early-morn-before-the-crack-of-sparrows stuff. And the Lie had long lost all its blondes and cheeries. Cheeky smiles had been replaced by bent and wizzened stoopings to protect itself, thin-lipped with the effort of just carrying on. ☞

The Lie's eyes became hollow pools of deep and darklies, where old cold secrets fester, its voice snarling the story now.

But no-one listened anymore. They'd heard it all before, had been 'urt and given up trying to be nice.

"Leave it alone," they'd say shaking their 'eads with sad contemplation that all could have been so different.

And now, when the Lie started to story to new people about this and that, no-one believed it anymore, 'cause the Lie looked too 'orrible, the truth showing so obviously on its face and through anything that it said.

In the end, the Lie couldn't 'urt no-one, no more. Except of course itself.

THE TOWERING BOGLE

Never rely on the Towering Bogle
As he oilingly greets you with warmingly slith,
Extending his hand, you'll marvel and ogle
And think you're so lucky it's him you are with.

He'll shower the compliment, laud and fete you,
Stoopingly smiling, it's part of his plan.
But deep down inside he'll really hate you
Because he can't do all the things that you can.

The Bogle is wily, the Bogle is clever,
Inveiglingly unctuous, appallingly vain.
But rely on the Towering Bogle? Never!
For he'll take your soul, as well as your brain.

So beware of the lair of the Towering Bogle,
For once in his clutches it's hard to resist.
The choice is yours: be free of the Mogul
Or slowly and surely cease to exist.

GRUNGE

When you're feeling grim and groggy,
Head's a-pounding, eyes are foggy,
Body aching, brain all soggy
So rotten that you'd kick the moggy –

Tough!!

SECTION FIVE

A

N

D

F

I

N

A

L

L

Y

.

.

.

TEN COMMANDMENTS

Don't wash,
Don't comb your hair,
Leave your clothes all over the stair.

Be late for school,
Don't eat your peas,
Never say pardon, thank you or please.

Write messy homework,
With blotches of ink.
Leave your pet froggie in the sink.

Let oil from your bike
Stain your best clothes,
And don't forget to pick your nose.

If all these things you can do,
Well all I can say is God Bless You!